Haiku for the Road

Haiku for the Road

STEPHEN HOLTON

Rivertowns BOOKS

ISBN-13: 978-1-7339141-9-2

LCCN Imprint Name: Rivertowns Books

Rivertowns Books are available online from Amazon as well as from bookstores and other retailers. Requests for information and other correspondence may be addressed to:

Rivertowns Books
240 Locust Lane
Irvington NY 10533
Email: info@rivertownsbooks.com

For my two grandfathers,
Werner Hans Bloch and Caryl Ames Holton

Haiku for the road:
a communion of words
for other travelers.

Contents

Introduction   1
Editor's Note   7

2020   9
2019   43
2017–2018   61
2013–2017   79

About the Author   105

Introduction

EACH MORNING AFTER WAKING, I sit down for a cup of coffee out on my deck or by an open window, and then, when sufficiently awake, settle into the silence and my morning meditation.

One day in 2013, in the middle of my morning prayer, words came into my head, suggested by creation all around, by the words upon my heart, and perhaps from a deeper source within every heart. I arranged them like puzzle pieces into a haiku format, an easy way to remember them, an elegant way to transmit them.

1

Since then, I have written almost three thousand haiku. They are like seventeen-piece puzzles arranged in three rows of five, seven, five. I put them in the package of a Facebook post for anyone to open.

Some are what I think of as morning prayer haiku—MPH for short—that "get me up to speed." These frame my day and provide a reference point from the undercurrent of my faith, not from the barrage of the world. When I get off track, I can refer back to them.

Others are snapshot haiku—words that frame a moment like a photograph. And some are reflection haiku when all my thoughts, often with Scripture to help me, come into focus.

As I write these haiku, I think of my Depression-era grandmother. She lived not far from the train station and put lovingly cooked meals on her window sill for passersby who were down on their luck. So I put these on the window sill of Facebook as nourishment for passersby in troubled times, as they continue on their way.

My Facebook friends are a helpful representation of our country today, and maybe these offerings can be helpful in our larger struggle to find our way as a nation. My friends include the military kids I grew up with around the world as a diplomatic kid. Many of them were evangelical Christians, which is how I found faith. My friends also include the liberal clergy I work with now. There are Muslims and Jews from my interfaith work. There are allies from rallies where I try to put my faith into action. There are beloved parishioners from the churches I have served. There are beautiful colleagues from my antiviolence work in Harlem. There are simply spiritual people who find a welcome in my words.

This goes to the larger purpose of sharing these posts. My dad always taught me to have the courage of my convictions. So if I go to a rally and do not post my feelings, perhaps I am ashamed of myself or them. If I have an experience of faith and do not share that, perhaps I am ashamed of that—but no.

In this way, I try to help bind our country a little closer together. I try to show that the divine can be known in city and country. Perhaps I show that, as diverse as we are, we are nourished by common spiritual food. Consistently, when I make some blessed posts that attract "likes" from people of every race and religion and spirituality, I have used words from Scripture or from God's other revelation— Creation. Apparently such words can nurture everyone.

There is a strong flavor of what I call donut haiku here, too. I learned the habit of afternoon coffee and a treat from my mom, who felt that if you did this every day, you could probably get through life. In donut shops, the ordinary people of God pause in the midst of their busy days. So I find God there, too, and I feel those haiku word blessings assembling themselves like pastries on a plate. Other word blessings assemble themselves in Sunday service Haiku, for often, at the altar, the simple joy of being a priest, proclaiming the faith in sweet fellowship, comes together in poetry.

Finally, my life with my wife, Charlotte, is the circle within which I am nourished most fully. You will see some haiku in which universal themes of marital life are reflected.

THIS BOOK IS THE PRODUCT of the encouragement of my editor, who first suggested gathering these haiku into a book and discerned the haiku of highest quality, pointing out the deeper, Godly surprises that lay just beneath their surface. Surprise, I've learned, is a hallmark of haiku. I never formally studied the art of haiku, although I'm sure I encountered it as a child when I lived with my family on diplomatic assignment in Japan. Perhaps, like many spiritual things, it waited until I was ready, and then became a container for spiritual communion from my life to yours.

The deepest surprise from that deepest source within us all is hope. I find it in our small towns and city neighborhoods. I am blessed to work in both. So I pass it on to those who are not so blessed.

Enjoy your journey. I hope these poems provide a little food along the road. The universal food of love, in every human heart from the heart of God, is worth sharing. It makes a communion of words, ordinary food that is offered with prayer by another traveler, who has found them useful and hopes you might, too.

Stephen Holton
White Plains, New York
January 2021

Editor's Note

THE HAIKU IN THIS BOOK are arranged in
reverse chronological order, from most recent to
oldest, just as you might encounter them on a
social media page. Thus, the poems in the first
few pages of the book offer flashes of life during
the turbulent year of 2020, a time of pandemic,
political division, and the "good trouble" of
popular uprisings on behalf of racial justice. As
you read on, you'll travel backward in time, as
you might if you were leafing through an old
diary.

Occasionally, I've chosen to include a brief
reference to the activity or place that inspired
the poem, a practice that probably violates the
principles of classic haiku. I suspect these

annotations will enhance your enjoyment of the poems, and I ask the indulgence of readers who notice that, in this way and others, the author and I sometimes choose to "color outside the lines" of traditional haiku practice.

I hope you'll find, as I have, that the best of these poems capture moments of insight, laughter, and grace that leave you with something timeless to savor and ponder.

Karl Weber
Irvington, New York
January 2021

2020

"Say Their Names" march in White Plains, New York,
June 21, 2020

There is a river
that flows through the world from God
bringing nourishment.

Reflection haiku • December 3

Wind blows through my hair;
tree says grow, water says flow
with beautiful sounds.

Reflection haiku • December 2

My two grandfathers—
German Jew, Methodist—
greet on native land.

Reflection haiku • October 19

Food of my people:
peanut butter and jelly
and a glass of milk.

Snapshot haiku • October 9

Like small knights they stand,
four little boys ready to
receive their blessing.

Sunday service haiku: Christ Church, Warwick
October 4

The earth is shaking
so give yourself to the wind
and blow over it.

MPH • October 2

After the battle,
God is the noncombatant
who welcomes us home.

MPH • September 30

As you go through life,
bring food from your faith and feed
other travelers.

MPH • September 29

Loving vibrations:
woman rocks child, and soon
her friends are rocking, too.

Snapshot haiku: Outside restaurant, Warwick
September 26

Zoom private struggle:
looking at everyone else
when I look so good.

Snapshot haiku • September 23

In our wilderness,
water flows from hard rocks
if you know where to strike.

Reflection haiku: Exodus lesson—water from the rock
September 22

Do not be afraid
of the world, but do not be
unprepared either.

MPH • September 21

Neighbors wave and cars
flash their lights to let me pass:
love at street level.

Snapshot haiku: My neighborhood • September 18

Online meetings mean
you can have wine and garlic
and no one will know.

Snapshot haiku • September 15

Every part of you
crystallized like diamonds
on God's lovely hand . . .

MPH • September 15

Come to the Lord
with your jumbled thoughts
and let them turn into Scripture.

MPH • September 11

Go in your weakness.
The Lord sends you to serve the
weakness of others.

MPH • September 10

Drumming our way home,
Muslim, Christian, African:
three drummers, one beat.

Snapshot haiku: Drum class in Harlem • September 9

Li'l kid plays in stream;
li'l fish—from another world!—
nibbles at his toes.

Snapshot haiku: A park in Warwick • September 6

In many cultures,
Jesus comes in many ways;
today, in crumb cake.

Snapshot haiku: Coffee and pastry in the East Village
August 28

The rich food of God
you find in God's presence
is meant to be takeout.

MPH • August 20

Just when you need it,
someone wakes up your heart
and helps it beat again.

Reflection haiku: Memorial for a friend in Warriors of the
Dream, Harlem—a group for meditation, drumming and
conversation • August 14

We don't really want
to be disturbed—but God
is a good disturbance.

MPH • August 11

What's in your hand—church?
Give it to the Lord
and it will feed 5,000.

Sunday sermon haiku: Adam Clayton Powell and Christ
Church, Warwick • August 2

Hearts are meant to break
and bring out the love inside
and the God inside.

MPH • July 31

You can find sweetness
if you look all around you—
ask a hummingbird.

MPH • July 28

In the bulrushes,
Moses stayed safe until he
came out a leader.

Reflection haiku • July 27

God, like a baker,
takes what you can offer
and makes it nourishing.

MPH • July 22

Ride the wave of God.
Let it carry you forward
to a distant shore.

MPH • July 16

Pandemic garden:
words of love you speak are seeds
that grow beautiful.

Reflection haiku: COVID-19 shelter-in-place • July 12

Be one with the Lord,
a center of gravity
for those lost in space.

Reflection haiku • July 19

The prayer kitchen:
bring every part of your life,
see what God cooks up.

Reflection haiku • July 5

Backyard fireworks and
mariachi bands tell me
freedom's still at home.

Snapshot haiku: Walking in my neighborhood
July 4

God breaks into an
incarcerated world so
he can break us out.

MPH • July 1

Wear a mask: protect
people from your toxic breath
and your ugly face!

Snapshot haiku • June 27

Hear the voice of God,
of pain, beauty, history:
Zoom room in Harlem.

Snapshot haiku: Peace Café Zoom • June 26

Take a deep breath
and step off the sidelines
into the presence of God.

MPH • June 24

Chipmunk hid from cat
behind Italian books;
left reading Dante.

Snapshot haiku: My bookshelf this morning • June 23

Your part of the web
depends on you to weave it.
Make it beautiful.

MPH • June 19

You are already there,
softened up and ready
to be made useful.

MPH • June 16

I know she loves me:
she makes me wear sunscreen
when I go to rallies.

Snapshot haiku • June 13

For the work today,
the Lord needs no perfect hearts:
you will do just fine.

MPH • June 9

Training in the woods,
my son punches out a tree.
All bark and no bite!

Snapshot haiku • May 28

When anger or pain
leaves you with nothing, then God
can make a good start.

MPH • May 28

Meanwhile, in Scotland,
the Word was made a tartan
and danced among us.

Reflection haiku: Scottish country dancing • May 21

Like a mama bird
bringing food to her young, God
brings hope each morning.

MPH • May 18

Front porch ministry:
have a beer, wave at neighbors . . .
playing to my strengths.

Snapshot haiku: In the time of COVID-19 • May 10

Leaving our temples,
we find God out in the world
and each other, too.

Sunday worship haiku: In the time of COVID-19
May 10

With no church today,
God gives takeout communion
through all creation.

Sunday worship haiku: In the time of COVID-19
May 10

Turtle said to me,
moving slowly through the woods,
"You're . . . on . . . the . . . right . . . track . . ."

Snapshot haiku: In the woods • May 6

In the edge places
beside roads and pandemics
God is still present.

Snapshot haiku: Wildflowers beside the road • May 4

In holy weakness
way out of our comfort zones
and way into God's.

MPH • May 1

Only faint breezes
fill your sails, but enough
to get you out to sea.

MPH • April 30

Birds of a feather
may flock together, but sheep
we just gotta love.

Reflection haiku: Good Shepherd Sunday • April 29

Connected by God
we rise . . . we fall . . . we are still
connected by God.

MPH • April 16

Was Thomas doubting
or too upset to believe?
Jesus can take it.

Reflection haiku: Scripture on Thomas • April 15

Like a grain of sand
in tiny communion
with the rest of the beach.

MPH • April 15

Like flowers each day
we still bloom, we still grow, still
draw strength from below

MPH • April 14

Lean in to this day,
rediscover the present:
the future can wait.

MPH • April 10

Because the Lord knows
dinner and conversation
begin a new world.

Reflection haiku: Passover • April 9

Chocolate cake mix
as if out of the darkness
arose before me . . .

Snapshot haiku: Stop & Shop • April 8

Always on the edge
between life and death—always
pointed to our God.

Reflection haiku: Muslims at prayer facing toward Mecca
April 8

Yearning for the Lord,
we lean through pleasure and pain:
anything for love.

MPH • April 6

Coronavirus:
with a viral crown of thorns
Jesus shares our life.

Reflection haiku: Palm Sunday • April 5

"What, there's no donuts?"
I cried out in my distress.
But they heard my cry!

*Snapshot Haiku: Panic at Westchester Greenhouse and
Farms • March 31*

A pillar of fire
can burn the whole house down
or lead you to freedom.

MPH • March 31

The trees aren't content
just to have branches, but grow
till they have flowers.

MPH • March 30

Light in a dark space
comes from life in a God space
transmitted by love.

Reflection haiku • March 27

Days of confusion:
we cannot see the Lord, but
we follow that voice.

MPH • March 26

Vulnerable Christ
tells Mary, "Do not touch me":
#FaithfulDistancing.

Reflection haiku: The news according to John 20:17
March 25

Breaking quarantine
for cat food and brownie mix:
only essentials.

Snapshot haiku: Stop & Shop • March 25

The spirit of God
blows us in new directions—
sails up, eyes open.

MPH • March 23

Social distancing:
flowers six inches apart
but still in God's earth.

Snapshot haiku: Planting flowers in the time of COVID-19
March 22

Hide and seek with God
Behind every tree you'll find
The Divine Presence

MPH • March 20

The power of words—
ancient technology
keeps us together.

MPH • March 20

The light of the world
has gone out of the temple
where it was crowded.

Reflection haiku: Coronavirus sermon • *March 19*

A bewildered world.
But I can still kiss my wife,
so . . . what's the problem?

Reflection haiku • *March 18*

Back to the basics:
Jesus healed a man with mud;
no special prayers.

MPH • *March 18*

Still small voice of love:
God's blessing since ancient times.
So call your neighbor.

MPH • March 17

Why have you been saved?
What paths of the past led you
to this moment here?

MPH • March 13

Do not be afraid
to walk in the dark, but learn
from those you find there.

MPH • March 12

A bright flame of love
can light up a whole room.
So go ahead and burn.

Sunday worship haiku: Scarsdale Friends Meeting
March 8

"Hear, O Israel"—
the first commandment of God:
simply to listen.

MPH • March 1

In the hands of God,
somehow all our broken bits
fit with all the rest.

Reflection haiku • February 28

Inner radiance
fills up with light from above.
The words are extra.

MPH • February 27

Locked in our prisons,
the Lord can find us, and we
cannot get away

MPH • February 26

Introvert's lament—
"Please don't make me talk to you"—
to all who pass by.

*Snapshot haiku: Mayor's reception at Museum of Natural
History • February 25*

The Lord welcomes us,
birds on the wing, to welcome
all the other birds.

MPH • February 23

God's ice-cream sundae:
more blessings than you can fit
in one tiny bowl.

Reflection haiku • February 21

Bring your sins to God.
See if they stink, and let God
take out the garbage.

MPH • February 19

Relieved-looking men
leaving the store tonight with
chocolates and flowers. ❤

Snapshot Haiku: Stop & Shop on Valentine's Day
February 13

Learning from wombats
how the rest of us survive
our devastation.

Reflection haiku: Australian fires, wombats welcome other
animals in their burrows • January 16

Pastry and prayer:
necessary nourishment
for my life's journey.

Snapshot haiku: Hungarian Pastry Shop near the
Cathedral • January 1

2019

St. Philips Church in the Highlands, Garrison, New York

Do not be afraid.
Just be—and that will give God
something to work with.

MPH • December 23

"We are family"
say the trees leaning toward me
In the evening light.

Snapshot haiku: Palisades Interstate Park
December 11

When we see what God
sees in each of us, we see it
in each other.

MPH • December 11

As wood fears the fire
and yet hungers to give life
so we fear the Lord.

MPH • December 6

Always on the edge
of our world but always in
the middle of God's.

MPH • November 18

For people and things,
not philosophical thoughts,
we give thanks, O Lord.

MPH • November 15

Don't ask for a sign.
Ask for a step and take it.
Firm ground for your feet.

MPH • November 14

Our broken spirits
can be made whole if we just
give God the pieces.

MPH • November 5

In a foreign land,
how do we sing the Lord's song?
Lots of rehearsal.

Reflection haiku • November 1

One elevator:
Jew with tzizim, my collar.
Two guys shine one light.

Snapshot haiku: Empire State Building • October 31

Squirrel said to me,
"To connect earth and heaven,
just keep on running."

Snapshot haiku: In the garden at the Cathedral
October 29

Don't travel alone:
if you go through a doorway,
invite others, too.

MPH • October 21

In the beginning,
God told a story,
and it began a new world.

MPH • October 20

She rolls her eyes as
her husband catches up:
that universal look.

*Snapshot haiku: Watching passengers at Leipzig Railroad
Station • September 28*

Carry your blessings
from the past to the future:
a fragrant perfume.

Reflection haiku • September 18

Be glue in the cracks,
softened, spread thin, and holding
it all together.

MPH • September 16

Found myself today
in a cinnamon muffin:
#ManyPathsToGod

Snapshot Haiku: Patio Restaurant, Briarcliff
September 2

When all you had was
a dixie cup of kindness:
"When I was thirsty."

Reflection haiku • September 8

A Q-tip of love:
small, but makes a difference
for someone who hurts.

Reflection haiku • September 4

In a stranger's smile,
God said I would get through what
I need to get through.

MPH • September 1

Like a poison pill,
God's word comes into our hearts
till they break open.

MPH • August 23

Holy restlessness
becomes forward movement when
you rest in the Lord.

MPH • August 22

The word of the Lord
will liberate us all from
the word of the world.

MPH • August 21

Open to the Lord,
we move into the future
with other nomads.

MPH • July 17

Support your weakness
with your strength until both
can act in partnership.

MPH • July 16

In the heart of an
incarcerated nation,
God comes with healing.

MPH • June 27

Latina Madre
asks me for my blessing and
so she blesses me.

Snapshot haiku: Washington Heights, Manhattan

June 5

On the road through life,
angels and car mechanics
help you on your way.

Snapshot Haiku: Silva's Auto Body, Elmsford
May 31

I finally see:
she asks my opinion
so she knows what won't work.

MPH • May 21

On the road through life,
you will have fender benders,
but the traffic still flows.

Snapshot haiku: Union Square, Manhattan • May 16

Like cherry blossoms,
we do not die when we fall
but adorn the earth.

Snapshot haiku: Cherry blossoms • May 9

Bring home your anger.
Jesus survived his passion;
he can survive yours.

MPH • April 26

After Jesus rose,
he did a little yard work.
That's when she saw him.

Sunday service haiku: St. Philip's, Garrison • April 21

The Lord will not rest
until you rise from your tomb,
blinking in the light.

MPH • April 9

Bird flies from the tree,
comes back for a safe landing.
Are you bird or tree?

MPH • April 1

Forgive me, dentist.
I have sinned: it's been two years
since my last visit.

Snapshot haiku: Greenburgh Health Center
March 25

From the burning bush
the Lord calls out to Moses:
"Since you're not busy . . ."

Sunday service haiku: St. Philip's, Garrison
March 24

After a long day,
learning of our divisions,
pizza makes us one.

Reflection haiku: After an anti-racism conference
March 16

In turbulent times,
don't take refuge from the storm:
learn to sail in it.

MPH • February 12

Put your whole self in:
we hokey pokey Christians
shake it all about.

MPH • February 5

Push through everything—
God, people, wind, rivers, all
push through death itself.

MPH • February 1

Crow spirit tells us
"There's something worth saving."
Maybe he's right.

Reflection haiku: Bear Mountain overlook • January 27

Even religion
becomes more useful
when you offer it to God

Reflection haiku: Wedding at Cana • January 17

Sooner or later,
a bridge has to settle on
both sides of the stream.

MPH • January 16

In a world of pain,
love each other like family.
Show what peace looks like.

*Snapshot haiku: Street Corner Resources shooting response
rally, Hamilton Heights • January 14*

After brokenness,
we become fluid, ready
to be something new.

MPH • *January 10*

2017–2018

Metro-North train station, New York City

Are you soft-hearted?
You're the one who can glue the
hard ones together.

MPH • December 7, 2018

If you look for love
in all the wrong places
you will still find it.

MPH • December 6, 2018

For any lost soul
there are always lost places
where God is waiting.

Snapshot haiku: Resting under a tree in a parking lot
November 19, 2018

It is the wanting,
it is the not giving up
that gets us to God.

MPH • November 19, 2018

The corner store
and breakfast with the neighbors
will be our salvation.

Snapshot haiku: Outside a deli • November 18, 2018

Learning from a scar:
don't try to heal too quickly,
just keep the wound clean.

Reflection haiku • October 9, 2018

The world is saved by
ordinary folks doing
ordinary things.

MPH • October 4, 2018

Down silent pathways,
God waits to be discovered . . .
playing hide and seek.

MPH • October 2, 2018

Pastoral drano:
when you throw love at a sin
and dislodge the clog.

MPH • September 19, 2018

The back of the world
keeps you safe from whatever's
happening in front.

MPH • September 18, 2018

Be like the fly who
brings garbage to the spider
who spins him to silk.

MPH • September 17, 2018

When nuns pass you by,
you know it from the plain clothes
and the peaceful breeze.

Snapshot Haiku: Ossining Pizzeria • August 2, 2018

As you exit, please
mind the gap between the train
and reality.

Snapshot haiku: New York City subway, Union Square
station • July 25, 2018

So tonight in prayer
God told me to have a beer
and play some Springsteen.

Reflection haiku • June 30, 2018

God told me in prayer
to go for a Greek coffee.
It seems to have worked.

Snapshot haiku: Lefteris Restaurant, Tarrytown
June 29, 2018

Who cares which came first?
From the egg comes a rooster
who proclaims the dawn.

MPH • June 27, 2018

Early one morning,
creation makes me a face
just to amuse me.

MPH • June 21, 2018

Best scene at wedding:
you know they're thorough when they
kiss in triplicate.

Snapshot Haiku: Wedding • June 9, 2018

Hard to talk with her
without going blind, seeing
her beautiful face.

Reflection haiku: Dinner with my wife • *May 8, 2018*

When God blesses you,
even old stick-in-the-muds
can grow new flowers.

MPH • *May 4, 2018*

On some days, I find
superficiality
deeply nourishing.

Reflection haiku • *April 21, 2018*

A specific grace:
"Lord, we give you thanks for steak
and also for beer."

Snapshot haiku: Dinner • April 30, 2018

Diversity note:
white men might work for freedom,
but we sure won't dance.

*Snapshot haiku: Poor People's Campaign rally
March 25, 2018*

God is a river
flowing throughout the whole world,
surfacing in us.

MPH • March 21, 2018

Who'd have thought Jesus
is present even in the
parochial report?

Snapshot haiku: St. James, North Salem
March 9, 2018

Throw yourself into
the mixing bowl of God's love
and see what comes out.

MPH • January 2, 2018

A voice cries to us:
"Mom says dinner's ready and
all is forgiven."

MPH • December 19, 2017

On Daddy's shoulders
she rides by, her eyes saying
"I'm queen of the world."

Snapshot haiku: Tom's Restaurant, Broadway
December 6, 2017

What does it mean that
you can give your worst to God
and it is still blessed?

MPH • September 29, 2017

Scottish country dance:
never turn your back on her.
It works for marriage, too.

Reflection haiku: Scottish country dancing
September 27, 2017

On broken altars
and faulty human beings
God rests anyway.

MPH • September 1, 2017

Choose whom you shall serve:
the god who keeps you safe, or
God who sends you out.

MPH • August 29, 2017

To be incomplete
means you must love your neighbor
to become yourself.

MPH • August 26, 2017

From frontier cultures—
Collins, Murkowski, McCain—
where you need neighbors.

Reflection haiku: Voting for the Affordable Care Act
July 28, 2017

Bring your Sunday worst,
give God something to work with,
become a blessing.

Sunday service haiku: St. James, North Salem
July 23, 2017

The utter mystery
of the presence of Christ is
a pain in the neck.

MPH • July 10, 2017

From many nations,
New Yorkers, forged into one
by subway delays.

Snapshot haiku: NYC subway • June 27, 2017

The Upper East Side:
even the trees introduce
themselves properly.

Snapshot haiku: Tree with nametag on it
June 26, 2017

I see her sitting
surrounded by her own light:
sunshine is wasted.

Snapshot haiku: My wife • June 23, 2017

Truck driver genius
navigates busy crossroads:
a good roll model.

Snapshot haiku • June 13, 2017

I prayed by the stream:
the water said "Keep moving."
How original!

Reflection haiku: In the woods • June 4, 2017

Words are paper-thin:
weave them into fabric
and they hold reality.

MPH • March 28, 2017

God is born again
in the womb throughout the world
there will be stretch marks.

MPH • March 13, 2017

It's a female voice
on my GPS. Sadly,
I never listen.

Snapshot haiku: #LostInTheBronx • March 3, 2017

Tried to bless my food.
Words wouldn't come, since it was
busy blessing me.

Snapshot haiku: Jacob Soul Food Restaurant, Harlem
February 20, 2017

Rumi's world and now
crush of empire presses out
mystic poetry.

Reflection haiku: Rumi book release, Cathedral
January 31, 2017

Keep our spirits up?
We don't have to, because God's
Spirit is down here.

MPH • January 25, 2017

Philosophically
I talk with my son. He thinks:
"Dear God, let me eat."

Snapshot haiku: Lunch at home • January 24, 2017

2013–2016

*Garden eucharist, St. James Episcopal Church,
North Salem, New York*

Look back carefully.
Many things have prepared you
for this moment now.

MPH • December 23, 2016

Ministry of dogs:
sit on sidewalk; sad human
stops, pats, starts smiling.

Snapshot haiku: Tom's Restaurant, Broadway
December 7, 2016

His eyes may be on
the sparrow, but these guys' eyes
are on my croissant.

Snapshot haiku: Sparrows at café • December 5, 2016

Here I am—send me
said the saints, without knowing
where they would be sent.

MPH • November 14, 2016

Sometimes the Spirit
comes as a dove, sometimes
the wild buffalo!

Reflection Haiku: Standing Rock • October 28, 2016

Kindled by God's love,
we're incandescent with love
and we won't go out.

MPH • October 25, 2016

"Grandma's rules" mean grace,
where no matter what you've done
you can still have pie.

MPH • October 7, 2016

Put out from the land
and all possible safety:
seabirds on the wind.

MPH • September 30, 2016

Don't fear your weakness:
just feel the contrast with
the strength of the Lord.

MPH • September 29, 2016

Incarceration:
the autocorrect Gospel
for incarnation.

MPH • September 18, 2016

See those pennants fly?
Today even the wind wants
to hear this music.

Snapshot haiku: Celebration in El Barrio
September 17, 2016

With ice cream blessings
after a hard day of school
he makes communion.

Snapshot haiku: Ice-cream cart in East Harlem
September 15, 2016

God offers us love
when all we have is anger.
We can use both.

MPH • August 31, 2016

I wait politely.
Kissing couple blocks the door.
This may take a while.

Snapshot Haiku: Tom's Restaurant, Broadway
August 24, 2016

Spirits fill bodies,
boys grow into pants too long.
God leaves room for growth.

MPH • August 24, 2016

Sometimes our anger
breaks counterfeit righteousness
to build the real thing.

MPH • August 3, 2016

Boy's best vacation:
smoking with his grandmother
in front of his mom.

Snapshot haiku • July 26, 2016

Lady in pink
walks by and shakes me to
a new reality.

Snapshot haiku • July 23, 2016

Who are we that we
should be the ones who bring God
to the world today?

MPH • June 16, 2016

God is all around,
sometimes observed shimmering
on leaves and people.

MPH • June 12, 2016

Perfect apple tart:
enough for me to love, but
not enough to share.

Snapshot haiku: Riviera Bakehouse, Ardsley
May 23, 2016

Life is not always
a journey to a goal but
a flower, blooming.

MPH • May 6, 2016

This is serious:
discussing "filioque"
over red wine—lots.

Snapshot haiku: Clergy at restaurant • May 4, 2016

The ancient structures
of prayer, work, shared food, and play
lead forward today.

MPH • May 3, 2016

Harriet Tubman?
Not in my wallet! She might
set my dollars free!

Reflection haiku: Putting Harriet Tubman on currency
April 20, 2016

God is a shepherd,
guiding us to good grass
even if we're baaad.

MPH • April 13, 2016

Like fishing vessels,
we seek what the Lord provides
beneath the surface.

April 6, 2016

Clueless competence:
that's how they know we're clergy.
We'll love anyone.

Reflection haiku: On being a priest • *April 5, 2016*

Fruits and vegetables . . .
oh, what the hell—cookies, chips—
and so the dam breaks.

Snapshot haiku: Stop and Shop • *April 2, 2016*

Thinking of haiku
makes snapshots of poetry
everywhere you look.

Snapshot haiku • *March 24, 2016*

Out here on the edge,
we can see past the mountains.
Baby steps get there.

MPH • March 15, 2016

Don't try to be big.
God uses small people to
get through a tight spot.

MPH • February 29, 2016

You don't have to be
fully present each moment.
That's God's job, not yours.

Sunday service haiku: St. James, North Salem
February 28, 2016

Excessive joy now—
we may not think it's useful,
but Jesus seems to.

Sunday service haiku: St. James, North Salem
January 13, 2016

Like puzzle pieces
misshapen and full of holes
we all fit right in.

MPH • January 6, 2016

Some parts of your heart
you can only enter with
some other dear one.

Reflection haiku • November 26, 2015

Water becomes wine.
Everything is possible
when nothing is left.

MPH • November 22, 2015

Sermon party mix:
throw in enough stuff, they might
find something tasty

Reflection haiku • November 21, 2015

When you're exhausted
and can no longer fight it,
your beauty comes out.

MPH • November 19, 2015

Newly deep voices
boom behind Halloween masks:
old boys playing young.

Snapshot haiku: Halloween • *October 31, 2015*

Not a lifeboat
or a pleasure cruise, the church
is a hospital ship.

MPH • *October 23, 2015*

Forget the future.
Grow roots, find strength, give birth:
it's all in the present.

MPH • *October 20, 2015*

Hold on to questions.
You don't get answers, but God
likes conversation.

Reflection haiku • September 20, 2015

The chicken did not
cross the road alone:
Jesus was with him.

Reflection haiku • July 23, 2015

The universe can
actually be counted on
to pick up the slack.

MPH • July 20, 2015

What happens when
you tell the old, old story
and see you're in it?

Reflection haiku: On Scripture • *July 19, 2015*

The Lord told David:
"Don't build a temple! That means
building committees!"

Reflection haiku • *July 14, 2015*

It is amazing
what you can accomplish when
you're not on Facebook!

Reflection haiku • *July 11, 2015*

The innermost point
of God's love is occupied
with small, tender things.

MPH • July 10, 2015

We find unity
in God's beauty, which enfolds
all distinctiveness.

MPH • July 6, 2015

Scatter the Gospel
everywhere. You never know
what grows among weeds.

MPH • May 20, 2015

In Gethsemane:
"Stay with me." Now stay with our youth
in our streets, one hour.

Reflection haiku: Vigil against Violence, Harlem
April 30, 2015

That part of you
that your spouse doesn't approve of
sometimes needs to lead.

MPH • March 13, 2015

Finally learning
not to say everything
that crosses my mind.

Reflection haiku • March 11, 2015

She ruffles his beard,
kisses him, and sends him off:
girlfriend's privilege.

Snapshot haiku: Tom's Restaurant, Broadway
March 11, 2015

Aimless and confused:
are they lost souls, or husbands
in the grocery store?

Snapshot haiku: Stop and Shop • February 28, 2015

Picked last for the team:
scrappy kids with mixed morals.
Just the kind God wants!

MPH • February 24, 2015

The church is a child,
screaming in uncertainty.
God says, "Use your Words!"

MPH • January 6, 2015

A powerful day:
I was slain in the Spirit,
then saved by caffeine.

Snapshot haiku: Coffee shop in White Plains
December 14, 2014

If Moses were French,
he would have cooked the frogs
with a little garlic.

Reflection haiku: On the Exodus • December 13, 2014

Will I stop crying
when I give out communion?
My God, I hope not.

Sunday service haiku: Christ's Church, Rye
December 7, 2014

God cares for us most
because we can't be trusted
with anyone else.

MPH • October 15, 2014

Make me a blessing,
but go easy on me, Lord.
"Sorry, no can do."

MPH • October 7, 2014

I write haiku since
I don't get paid by the word,
just the syllable.

Reflection haiku • September 20, 2014

It is the morning,
a time for new dreams and for
old ones well rested.

MPH • May 19, 2014

There comes a point when
God takes away your faith and
God alone is left.

MPH • December 29, 2013

Grace is a puppy
that will not give up on you.
It just wants to play!

MPH • November 1, 2013

I'm learning about
intercessory prayer
now that my son can drive.

Snapshot haiku • September 14, 2013

You are the garden
where God walks in the evening.
Leave the gate open.

MPH • September 11, 2013

Jesus broke the rules,
even the ones we're good at.
How irritating!

MPH • August 1, 2013

Foxes have holes and
birds have their nests, but I have
my own lawn to mow.

Reflection haiku: New homeowner • June 27, 2013

About the Author

MY STORY REALLY BEGINS with my two grandfathers—a German Jew and an Ohio Methodist—who met when my mother and father married. My German Jewish grandfather fled Nazi Germany with his wife and daughter, my mother, in the 1930s seeking freedom. My Ohio Methodist grandfather welcomed them to this land; to which his own family had come in the 1630s, also seeking freedom. This mutual welcome happened on beautiful Native American land that nourishes me daily when I walk in the woods.

I grew up around the world because my father was a U.S. diplomat who with my mother represented our country. With my brother and sister, I lived in six different countries. The constant in our household, in every country, was family dinner. At the end of the day we gathered, sharing conversation over our meal, generally with music in the background.

I was ordained to the Episcopal priesthood in 1989. I married that same year and with my wife and sons have lived in four different parishes—one long-term position in Ossining, New York, and three interim positions, also in the Hudson Valley.

The constant in our household has always been family dinner. At the end of the day we gather, sharing conversation over our meal, often with music in the background. The constant in my parishes has been another kind of family meal—Holy Eucharist (followed by coffee hour). At the end of every week, on a Sunday morning, we gather, sharing Scripture and sermon, with music (in the foreground).

After my position in Ossining, I returned to seminary to study the roots of our Episcopal identity. Not surprisingly for me, I saw how, going back to the ancient monasteries, we have gathered for food, music, Scripture, and sacred conversation, in every land and culture.

Based on this knowledge, I formed a group called Warriors of the Dream in Harlem, with drums for the music. It led to some sacred conversation. The dream is Martin Luther King's dream—a dream of gathering in beloved community, seeking freedom. I work with friends of many faiths, finding nourishment in their partnership.

THERE IS A STREAM that runs through the woods behind my house. Every morning, I clear it of twigs and trash so the water can flow free. My Jewish family flowed free on the waters of God. My Christian family welcomed them farther downstream. The waters of God carried my family around the world, and carry my family today. We disperse every day, then gather every night sharing conversation. My churches do the same. My friends do the same.

I wrote my first haiku as texts to my son in college. They were shorter than a phone call and, I thought, a bit more meaningful than an email:

> An elegant way
> to communicate—in verse
> using just your thumbs.

That first haiku washed up on my son's cellphone screen, carrying a thought, beginning a conversation. You're welcome to join in.

S.H.